How to start
An Insurance Agency and Brokerage Guidebook.

By Michael Bonilla

"All growth depends upon activity. There is no development physically or intellectually without effort, and effort means work." – Calvin Coolidge

About the Author.

My name is Michael Bonilla. I'm a former insurance Agent/broker and current consultant for insurance agencies. I've written about a dozen books on varying insurance topics. My books are not known for their grammatical structure, just the content. My aim with each book is to relay complicated concepts in simple ways. If we can find an easy way to have a hard conversation, that to me is a successful book. Buying insurance doesn't have to be some arduous and complicated process. But, sometimes we perceive it that way and that is really why I like to write about insurance.

Preface

This is the second edition of this book and I took a very different approach. After receiving some invaluable constructive feedback, I made an adjustment. Firstly, I added about 10,000 words. Secondly, I thought about all of the things that no one taught me when I started my agency from scratch. I thought about all of the problems, challenges and misadventures that I faced. I've added and redacted aspects of the book that newer Agency owners requested. I've also infused some case studies and adapted the content to reflect both Captive and Independent Owners. This book is geared towards multiline Agency owners and personal lines agency owners. This book will not touch on health insurance and very little on commercial liens insurance. No matter what you think of this book please leave me some feedback. But, do me this favor, read the entire book before leaving that feedback.

Table of Contents

- About the Author. 3
- Preface 4
- Why do you want to be an Insurance Agent? 6
- Common Questions, Challenges and Myths 9
- Introduction 20
- Landscape of the Industry 32
- Consumer Segmentation 59
- Marketing 67
- Sales Tips & Rules 112
- Book of Business Valuation 123
- What do You Need to Get Started? 139
- Business Plan 144
  - SWOT Analysis 144
  - Mock Start up Financial Statement 152
  - Premium Forecast and Commission Forecast .154
  - Budget 155
- Summation 171

Why do you want to be an Insurance Agent?

In my consulting practice, I like to ask Agents or prospects thinking about becoming Agents one simple question. Why? Why do you want to be an insurance agent? This is the most important question in the book and this will be the most important question you'll ever have to ask yourself. Most people don't plan on becoming an insurance agent. Most people don't grow up and have dreams of selling auto policies. For most people we kind of just fall into the industry. Either a friend recruits us, a family member owns an Agency or we take a summer internship. However you end up here, remember these simple words from Merry Riana, "With a big enough why, how usually doesn't matter."

Why do you want to start an Agency? For most people, myself included, it was the temptation of freedom. What I mean by that is as an Agency owner you have a lot of freedom. Why is that? Because, our business generates residual income through policy renewals. So, I urge you, as you read this book, as you start your practice, figure out what your reason is. Figure out your why.

Why do you think I'm putting so much emphasis on this topic? Owning an Insurance Agency isn't like owning other businesses. It requires a tremendous amount of sacrifice and front end work to build. What if I told you that only about 5% of Insurance Agents are able to make it? Would that change your mind? Would you put that into your calculation? Would you start looking at real estate instead of insurance?

Here are a couple of questions to ponder as you begin your exploration into becoming an insurance agency owner:

- Why would you make a good insurance broker/agent?
- What do (would) you like about being an agency owner?

- How did you decide to own an agency?
- What made you explore the opportunity?
- Did you have an insurance Agent before?
    - If so, why or why not?

Ask yourself this very important question.

Do you have $300,000 worth of premium within your immediate network? What I mean is do you know enough people who would buy insurance from you, because of you? If you start from scratch remember people are not going to just magically call you out of the blue for an insurance quote, people aren't going to wonder into your office one day hoping that you can quote their auto and home insurance.

Common Questions, Challenges and Myths

Common Misconceptions and Insurance Myths

1. **Millennials all buy insurance over the internet.** Why is that? Because, you're 60 years old! I hear this excuse all the time. "Millennials don't value insurance, etc., etc." Why? Because, we don't know how to reach them effectively. If you believe this common myth, let me ask you:
   - How often do you post useful information on Twitter, Facebook, Instagram, etc.?
   - Do you have a Twitter, Instagram, etc.?
   - Do you know what Twitter, Instagram, etc.?
   - When was the last time you received a quote request on Yelp?
   - Do you know you have a yelp?
   - What is your Google Ads budget?

- How often are you running email drip campaigns?
- Do you have a social media management platform and content provider?
- Do you know what your website click-thru-rate is?
- Do you have a website?
- How often do you update your website?
- What is your highest trafficked hour/day on your website?
- What is your digital marketing strategy?
- What is your video marketing strategy?

Can you answer ALL of these questions? If not, it's not surprising you are not acquiring younger customers. If you don't communicate in the channels that people live in, you won't be able to reach them. Who is communicating and advertising in the millennial channel? The internet companies, because they advertise on the internet! What does your website look like? The direct writing companies are dominating and have been dominating this space for the last decade.

2. **People do not want to come in the office.** Again, this is a common myth I hear a lot of people complain about. Well people really don't care about insurance and want things done quickly. This is true if you let it be true. This is true for a certain segment of the market. Again, let me ask you:
   - What attempts have you made to meet them at the office?
   - What attempts have you made to have them meet at their home?
   - What attempts have you made to meet them at a coffee shop on the weekend?

3. **All people care about is price, pure and simple**. You're right. No one cares about protecting their stuff, they only care about the cost it requires to protect their stuff. Don't fall into the price trap. It's easy to become disenfranchised in this industry and fall into the race to zero or the race to the bottom of constant price shopping.

All people care about is what you ask them to care about. This is why asking questions is so important during the buying process. This is also why setting expectation is also extremely important during your presentation and fact finding. If you presentation is, "I'm going to shop the market for you and every year shop for you." You're doing twice as much work as necessary, one because you haven't even asked the client what they care about protecting and two your attrition will actually be higher as you are prom[ting them to shop. Focus on protection and focus on value.

4. **My Insurance Company Isn't Competitive.** This by far is the biggest complaint and misnomer agents tell me. The question isn't whether your insurance company is competitive or not. It's rather, do you fully understand where your insurance company is competitive and when? Every insurance company is competitive for a certain segment of the marketplace. You know how we can tell? Because, THEY ARE STILL IN BUSINESS AND WRITING NEW BUSINESS!!! What I've found is that this is a mindset problem and a problem of motivation. But. Mike my insurance company only closes 7% of cases... so... what's your point? Okay, you have to quote 15 prospects to close one account. That's quite an acquisition cost, but what's the alternative? Sit around and do nothing?

Common Challenges

Here at the most common challenges you will face as a new agent and even as an existing agency owner.

- Building a culture of production and retention.
- Meeting carrier production demands and profitability goals.
- Transitioning from a liquidation mindset to a growth mindset.
- Producers not producing.
- Finding time to work on the business and not in the business.
- Convincing consumers to think about value over price.

Common Agent Questions

- How do I show a client I care?
    - Learn to ask open ended questions. I will address this heavily later on in the book.
- How do I get clients into the office?

- o Addressed above.
- Should my CSR/CSA be selling? If so, why?
    - o Yes, because each employee you hire should be profitable. You are running a business not a charitable organization.
- How do I get my CSR to Sell?
    - o Incentive structured compensation programs for both cross-selling/New Business/Retention, proper cross selling systems and time management skills via time blocking. That's it.
- How do I get my producer to produce?
    - o First, understand you must provide them with leads.
    - o Secondly, look at a small base salary on top of commission. In the long run this has a higher success rate and it will be more profitable for you.

- Why don't my employees seem to care as much as I do?
    - Most likely you are paying a fixed compensation. Which means you are not providing bonus opportunities and no or little commission and or providing fixed bonuses for sales that do no scale properly.
    - Also, understand no one ever will care as much as you, not even business partners you might bring on. This is your dream. This is your baby so to speak.
- How do I sell on value and overcome price as a focus?

- The customer will focus on what you focus on. If all you talk about is price, then all the customer will talk about is price. How is a home the most important financial asset a family can own, but people squabble over paying for a $5000 deductible. Shift the conversation. Price is merely the cost of value. Sometimes you need to have a tough conversation and ask questions.

Introduction

After managing, owning, selling and overseeing hundreds of Agencies you tend to pick up a few best and worst practices Agencies implement. Let me as you some questions:

- Are you thinking about starting a career in the insurance industry?
- Or perhaps you are thinking about switching companies or selling your Agency?
- Or possibly have you found yourself stuck in a rut in the age of automation?

Surprisingly both Agents and Brokers face the same three big challenges; staffing, selling/marketing insurance and retention.

So, in this book we are going to tackle common problems Agents run into and uncommon solutions. There is a science to running an insurance agency and a lot of these pieces of advice seem like common sense but are rarely common practice.

What I've found was that most Agents although appreciative of advice, rarely ever implement that advice.

The days of isolated pockets of 'general-experts' has come and gone. Having a niche and providing value is the future of insurance agencies/brokers. With automation and the internet it's easier now than ever for a customer to shop and find a lower premium.

Success leaves clues and successful people will tell you how they became successful. So I learned to listen and find these clues. We went from an Agency with no standards and a broad product line to an extremely narrow focus. We shrunk our product offering down and focused on knowing those narrow lines better than the competition.

We became number one on the world's largest rating/search engine because of these systems and processes. Then with a lot of consideration we sold out. So read this knowing there is not one absolute best way to run an Agency.

Calvin sun describes the four stages of learning as such:

Stage 1 – Unconscious Incompetence. You are unaware of what you don't know. (Brand New Broker/Agent/Producer)

Stage 2 – Conscious Incompetence. You are aware that you need to learn more.

Stage 3 – Conscious Competence. You can complete a task and know that you can complete a task with vert minimal assistance.

Stage 4 – Unconscious Competence. You can tie your shoes without thinking about how to tie your shoes.

At the very least this book will give you some kind of spark or inspiration. Maybe you take away a system or a process that can move you from one stage to another. Take something away from this book and make it your own and discard the rest.

But Mike, aren't insurance agents a dying breed of the past?

Yes and No. Fifty percent of millennials are buying insurance directly online. But, with insurance like anyone reading this book knows, what you don't know might hurt you financially. Not all insurance policies are made the same and different risks require different coverage. As long as you offer value, this industry will most likely be around for a long while.

But Mike, What does an Insurance Agent actually do?

Surprisingly, I get this question quite a lot. Mostly from insurance agents struggling to compete against the rising tide of online-direct writers. It depends on the kind of Agent you become. The key purpose of an Agent is to solve a problem for a customer.

For instance, the customer is shopping price and you like to save people money. Or the customer is concerned about not having the right coverage and you educate them and provide customized solutions.

An Agent can still add value in the insurance buying process, because the process is not fun, easy and or at the least bit simple to understand. Customers don't understand what they have or what they have at stake if a loss occurs.

Agents/Brokers can provide the following...

- Shop the insurance market.
- Field Underwriting
- Assess Risk and Uncover Gaps
- Offer a Personal Touch and humanize the insurance buying process.
- Offer After Hours / Weekend Service

- Offer customized Product Design based around Solutions for clients.
- Education – is the foundation to adding value.
- Act as an Advocate during the claims process.
- Act as an Advisor during the claims process.
- Negotiate and Work thru the Subrogation Process.
- Provide Risk mitigation advice and guidance.
- Table Shavings for life insurance.
- X-Mod assistance.

If you want to be an effective insurance agent, these above referenced activities are just that, activities. As a strategy at a high level our job is notice things. Our job is to be observant and ask questions. Analyze data and help insured's make adjustments to their current risk management program. If you notice some gaps let the insured know and call it out. Hey John, I noticed that your home insurance seems a bit low. Why is that?

What is our job?

Is our job to be personal shoppers? Maybe, but maybe it's more impactful than that. Maybe it's to really be trusted advisors and provide guidance. When I run training courses I like to ask these kinds of questions and really get people to think about what it is they do. Why is their job important? Why does it matter? Why should it matter?

A.M. BEST RATINGS

What is A.M. Best?

From A.M. Best, "A.M. Best was founded in 1899 by Alfred M. Best with the mission to report on the financial stability of insurers and the insurance industry. It is the oldest and most widely recognized provider of ratings, financial data and news with an exclusive insurance industry focus."

Why is it important?

An A.M. Best rating is an opinion based on financial criteria. That being said, the A.M. Best rating system is the gold standard of insurance rating systems and can be strong indicators of financial stability of an insurance company. This matters because, as a broker you represent the client and if you're willing put a client with a financially inadequate insurance carrier, you can be sued for negligence.

What are the ratings?

- **A++, A+, A, and A-** all identify the **top insurance companies**. Receiving an A for the company shows how financially strong they are, how capable a company is of guaranteeing your policy and keeping it secure.

- **B++, B+, B, and B-** ratings rank companies as good for those who can't afford what higher ranked companies offer their services for. With a B ranking you can depend on the company to provide a secure policy for affordable rates and rely on them to help your family get the help they need once you're gone. For client's knowing that your family has something to fall back on during difficult times is a welcome relief.
- **C++ and C+** are the only two scores for the C category, indicating an average insurance company. No bells or whistles attached, just a straightforward policy with straightforward premiums, a great choice for the first time you buy life insurance.
- A '**D**' rank is only reserved for companies that fall below A.M. Best's minimum standards, an E rank means the company is under state supervision, and

an F rank is only for companies going into liquidation. Any rating below a C shows how unreliable the company with in the industry.

Competitor Intelligence

There are three easy and reliable sources to gather competitor intelligence.

- Industry Trade Shows and Events
- Department of Insurance Rate Filings
- Colleagues and Marketing Reps

As an agent and as a broker gather and collecting competitor Intel is crucially important to proper marketing and planning. How do you know where your low hanging fruit are? For instance, if you have a follow-up quotes not closed campaign and ABC Insurance files for a 26% rate increase, those may be your high value targets.

Industry Trade Shows and Events

Tradeshows are great ways to get facetime

with prospective carriers and agency management companies. Tradeshows often are great sources of new trends, funding companies and general networking opportunities.

Department of Insurance Rate Filings

Pulling the rate filings on a regular basis can be a huge asset to your marketing efforts. Often agents ask me when to follow up with Quotes not sold and I say, when their carrier takes rate or every 9 months. Why every 9 months? Because, that is normally when the insured gets the rate indication for the renewal. The department of insurance is a breadth of information and one of the most valuable pieces of information is the rate indication for the DOI. Which shows what the DOI thinks ABC insurance company needs to increase their rates by in the short term to midterm.

Colleagues and Marketing Reps

Your colleagues and industry connections can be great sources of information about changes in the industry and not to mention great referral sources.

Insurance Facts

- 9 out of 10 youth fatalities happen between May and august.
- 25% of claims are reported after hours.
- Average cost of a new car is $30,000
- Rental car limits of $30 a day = Toyota Camry
- 75% of accidents take place within 25 miles of your home.
- For every $1000 in damage you can expect about 1 day of repair time.

Landscape of the Industry

Our industry is at a cross roads. Direct writer (online insurance companies) are chewing up market share and dominating the online distribution channel. We are at something I often to refer as the 'Great Protection' crisis.

Why? Insurance ownership is at an all-time low. There is a giant race to zero going on and people are forgetting what insurance is for. Insurance is not a commodity. It's the greatest social good ever created and yet for some reason only 60% of households have life insurance. On top of that at least 50% of drivers have either no insurance or not enough insurance.

The Chamber of Commerce estimates that there are nearly 1,000,000 licensed insurance agents/brokers, producers and Customer Service Reps in America. There are two types of Agents we will discuss in the chapter. Captive Agents and Non-captive Insurance Agents. Usually captive agencies have great training programs and require a certain amount of capital to start. Captive Agencies are similar but not the same to starting a franchise. Captive Agencies hold a large percentage of market share of insurance market.

Captive Agencies: are captive to one parent insurance company. Meaning they have a single company and products under the roof of that company or a subsidiary company.

State Farm – State Farm has a captive Agency model where Agents manage the book of business and work for State Farm as employees of State Farm. State Farm is the largest captive insurance company.

- **AM Best Rating:** A+
- **Gross Written Premium**: $63.9 Billion

Allstate – Allstate has a captive Agency

model. Allstate is the second largest captive insurance company and a stock insurance company. Allstate owns multiple subsidiary companies. Allstate has a great track record of claims service and an extremely broad product line to help Agents succeed. Allstate is way ahead of the curve for captive agencies for adopting insure-tech and innovative solutions for consumers.

- **AM Best Rating:** A+
- **Gross Written Premium:** $35 Billion

Farmers – Farmers has a captive Agency model, but Agents with no available markets can write insurance outside of the Farmers network, depending on whether Farmers has a secondary network or offers the product. Farmers is owned by Zurich and also has capital requirements for new Agencies.

- **AM Best Rating:** A+
- **Gross Written Premium:** $19 Billion

American Family – American Family is another captive insurance agency model. American Family has a similar business model to Allstate or State farm. American Family is a fast growing captive insurance company with a stronger presence on the east coast.

How do I chose a Captive Carrier?

There isn't an easy answer to that question. Each company offers something unique and different. Each company will have a consultant or marketing rep that will be more than happy to speak about the opportunity. Start by asking yourself a few questions.

- What's the reputation of that carrier?
- What does that carrier do well?
- What doesn't that carrier do well?
- What do you want to do?
- What is the carrier asking me to do?
- How much ownership do I have of the book of business?
- What does the contract look like?

- What amount of capital do I have to put up front?

Non-Captive Agents/Brokers: Non-captive agents simply represent more than one insurance company and are considered independent.

But Mike, What's the difference between an Agent and Broker?

An insurance Agent represents the insurer by definition. Whereas an insurance broker represents the insured. A captive insurance agent typically can only represent and write with a single insurance company. Most captive insurance carriers have outside markets and more than one underwriting company.

The main difference is that an Agent has retroactive binding authority and can act on behalf of the insurer. Agency contracts prohibit broker fees whereas Brokers often charge fees.

Brokers can have both Agency and Broker contracts with insurance carriers. To charge broker fees you must be licensed and bonded.

But Mike, Should I be captive or Independent?

The answer is that there is no one way of doing things. I know Agents of all sizes and of all kinds. What I can say for certain is that you should do your research and talk to the different companies to see what the right fit would be for you. I've operated in both spheres and they both have different advantages and disadvantages. Do your research and make an informed decision.

Aging Industry

In my opinion there is no better time to enter this industry. Our industry has aged. Aged to the point that by 2020 about half of the industry will arrive at retirement age. For acquisitions and growth, now is the time to enter this industry. According the U.S. Bureau of Labor Statistics, over the next few years we can expect that around 400,000 employees will be retiring.

But Mike, how much can I charge for a broker fee?

The department of insurance recommends you charge no more than 10% of the premium and always for ethical purposes keep the fees consistent.

REQUIREMENTS per the Department of Insurance

In order to charge a broker fee, a broker must meet the following requirements:

The consumer agrees to the fee in advance, after full disclosure.

The fee is not being charged on a CAARP, FAIR Plan, or "Low Cost Auto" policy.

The broker is not an appointed agent of the insurer with which the coverage is or will be placed.

The broker provides the consumer with a specific disclosure form.

The consumer and broker sign a broker fee agreement containing certain standard information.

The broker has an in-force broker bond on file with the Department.

The broker discloses the existence of the broker fee at the time of the initial premium quotation.

But Mike, how do I get started in the independent channel?

There are hundreds of companies in the independent agent channel that an independent agent or broker can offer. The independent channel has the majority of the premium in the insurance market.

Also, depending on the state a lot of insurance companies go in and then go out. So, the landscape is changing constantly and commission rates with independent companies tend to change as well. The new shift in the industry if moving towards variable commissions.

The two ways for someone to start in the independent channel:

- Seeding Program
  - Partnership
  - Book buy
- Starting From Scratch

A seeding program is simply you working for an Agency and either crafting one of two agreements with that agency. One option is that you seed in and contract to buy out your book of business. In that, you build your book of business under someone else who holds appointments. This makes sense for both parties because the agency gets a cut of your commissions and you get to learn the business with no financial recourse or risk. Also, the agency owner gets a big pay day when you buy back your book of business from the producer.

A seeding program can also work where you start fresh and partner up with an existing established agency to one day either acquire the business and or just be partners in perpetuity.

Starting from scratch is what I did, and in California it was an education in what I did not know. Luckily, I learn very quickly, as I tend to sprint into my own mistakes and missteps.

But Mike, If I start a scratch independent Agency how do I get carrier appointments?

Some carriers will give you a shot as a scratch agency, but very few will ever consider it as a possibility. Having a well thought out business plan and center of influence never hurts. Most insurance companies look at it as a business case. What is your primary lead source? What is your history in the industry? Where are you going? But, if you don't have a strong marketing plan or source of leads, you can always look into General Agencies or Managing General Agencies or Aggregators.

Ask for referrals and learn the good and the bad about working with each type of company. Do your research and make an informed decision as the contracts for most Aggregators come with a lot of strings attached. Some aggregators come with no strings so make sure to do your research. Ask a lot of questions before making any commitments or big decisions as you could get buyer's remorse. Some questions to ask:

- What are my commissions?
- What are the costs?

- Who owns the book of business?

But Mike, is it easy to start an Insurance Agency?

Easy is never an option. This is a business like any other business. If you come in with capital and structure then the odds are you come out with a profit. If you expect that people will magically just buy insurance from you... Good luck! The first year is rough, I'm not going to sugar coat it. But, when the second year rolls around and you start to see those residual checks, it gets easier. That growth compounds and if you scale properly you will have a very successful business up and running in a few short years.

Current M&A landscape

Agencies are selling like hotcakes these days. One because there are a tremendous amount of people retiring, but also because it's a lot easier from a customer acquisition standpoint to just absorb smaller agencies.

Customer acquisition for agencies is around $300 per account by most guesses. There are also large aggregators making very generous offers on book of business and agencies. When we put our agency up for sale we received 15 offers in two days. One offer even included gold bullion as an enticement, obviously that we did not go with.

If you plan on buying an agency or brokerage we can dig into that topic further into the book. But, just remember do your research before making any decisions.

But Mike, What else should I consider if starting from scratch?

Selling insurance is easy for the most part. The tough part is having enough people to sell to. So, think long and hard about people who would be willing to buy insurance from you.

Who are the customers you want to serve?

There are three kind of risk profiles for customers in the insurance market. Sub-standard, Standard and Preferred clients.

Sub-standard: the Sub-standard market is a market that usually a very consumer fluid market place. Typical consumers have lower PIF per household with one agency and very low retention. Sub-standard Auto for instance generally requires a higher degree of administrative work and commissions are usually lower.

Standard: Usually low claims frequency and shops regularly.

Preferred: The preferred market is a market where consumers shop infrequently and have low and no claims frequency. The preferred market generally hold a higher self-insured retention in comparison to other types of customers. Highest customer loyalty of the three categories.

But Mike, which type of customer should I serve?

It depends. What's congruent with the type of agency you want run? What does your insurance company offer? Also, determining which type of client you want to serve will help narrow your focus.

The importance of selecting or considering selecting a target market is so you can define your practice and choose a product selection.

It's a lot easier to figure out who you have access to and then select a product offering than select a product offering and hope those corresponding people will congregate towards you as an agent. Don't put the cart before the horse. For instance are you getting 90% of your traffic from an Estate Attorney? Maybe you should offer life insurance?

But Mike, Should I have a narrow focus if I am brand new to the industry?

This is a question I get a lot. The answer is you have to make a choice. You have to choose from being a generalist or a specialist. Know a lot about a little or a little about a lot. As an Agent you will have a wide variety of choices of products you can offer. It's easy to get tempted to find a market to place business if you get a lead.

I was of the opinion (after some growing) to farm out business I was not an expert in to grow my professional network and develop referral sources. If I had an obscure lead I would try to find a specialty broker who could in return send me business.

Even if your parent company offers

many products think about specializing in one of those products so you can stand out from your competition.

Also, think about this. If you decide to only offer X but are only getting Y type clients. Maybe you should change your focus.

Choosing Insurance Offerings

So, once you've figured out who you sign up with. It's time to figure out what kind of products you want to offer. So here are some of the options.

Property and Casualty

Personal insurance: Automobile, Collector's Auto, Home Insurance, Dwelling Fire Insurance, Renters insurance, Umbrella Insurance, Personal Liability, Motorcycle Insurance, Recreational Vehicle, All Terrain Vehicle Insurance, Boat Insurance, Yacht Insurance, Condo Insurance.

Commercial Insurance: Surety Bonds, Business Insurance, General Liability, Workers Compensation, EPLI, Surplus Lines, Marine Article Floaters, Commercial Auto, Commercial Umbrella Insurance,

Life Health and Annuity

Life Annuity and Health: Group Life, Group Annuity, Group Health, Decreasing Term, Level term, Hybrid Term, Return of Premium Term, Indexed Universal, Variable Universal Life, Guaranteed Universal Life, Universal Life, Long term care, Group and Individual Health, Disability, Vision and Dental.

The Importance of having a coach.

The only way I was able to make adjustments and adapt to grow my business was by making mistakes. Luckily I made them all relatively quickly and learned and adapted. I liked to think of it like breaking something and then learning to put it back together.

What helped me during that learning process was having good mentors and learning from the experience of others. It's easy to take that advice and think you have to reinvent the wheel. You don't have to reinvent the wheel. What I liked to do was learn the best processes and systems and then make small adjustments to fit my style of communication. But, for the most part I would keep the framework the same.

One of my main areas of prospecting was on the golf course. What you learn quickly in golf is that you need to learn to adhere to and perfect a process in order to be consistent and then become good. Selling insurance or owning an agency is a process no different than learning how to swing the club.

But, it's important to have someone show you the way and hold you accountable. You can learn to 'golf' by yourself and maybe become a scratch golfer one day or you can have someone show you the way.

Staffing an Insurance Agency

There are many different ways to staff an agency and compensate your staff. I've tried them all, and believe me there is no silver bullet that is plug and play for every agency. What I found to be most effective from experience is a combination of fixed and variable pay, for every employee in my firm.

But Mike, for every employee?

Why not? But, remember every Agency is different. What might have worked for mine might not work for yours. The reasoning behind that kind of model was simple. I tried high percentages of commission and low or no fixed pay. This obviously is how we all started as agents, but your producers and marketing people are not business owners.

What you get with variable pay is accountability and incentive to grow/push. My thought process was I wanted each employee or contractor to care about losing a client as much as gaining a client, the easiest way for me to do that was by making it so they had a stake in the game.

Consider this:

1. Sharing Profit Bonuses
2. Sharing company specific production campaign bonuses.
3. Having a Retention Bonus
4. Paying Residual Commissions to Employees.

Not Every Employee is created equal.

There is no one cookie cutter plan for compensation you can pull out of a book and implement. Some employees are motivated by money. Some by work/life balance and enjoyment of the job. Some like the work environment. Some employees value praise from immediate supervisors. Some just want that money.

If you choose to try out a somewhat variable compensation plan you are providing a structure that allows for personal and business growth. Your top performers will keep being top performers and your steady eddies will keep being consistent, because they are incentivized to grow and keep producing.

The only wrong answer is that there is only one right answer for compensation models. So, if it works it works. Test. Gather Results. Make adjustments where needed. Rinse and Repeat.

As a side note if you choose to revamp you pay schedules for producers/CSR/AM you will most likely receive some push back.

But Mike, why not pay my producers all commission?

There is a minimum amount of money

each employee has to bring home in a paycheck to justify a keeping a job. Most commission sales people fail. Plain and Simple. Because, they lack the marketing resourcefulness to keep their funnel full of prospects.

So, if you decide to pay commission only, you'll find a high turn-over. Commission only is generally less risky of a proposition as you make outlays only if the producer sells, but if they are desperate to sell they might produce poorly written business just to make money. Figure out what works for your existing infrastructure and see what works.

But Mike, When should I hire employees?

If you could sum up an employee in a single statement of purpose, "To make my managers job easier and make my company money." So ask yourself that question. At what point does your capacity plateau to where you need some help to grow?

Should I do Business over the phone/email?

There are different schools of thoughts. Most people like to do business thru the modality they choose. So some people want to buy insurance via email and E-signatures. Some people want to buy insurance thru a mobile app. Some people like to look around online and then talk to an actual person.

JD Power runs a study each year for Insurance Consumer shopping habits. The study found in 2016 that 74% of consumers use insurer websites or aggregators for obtaining quotes and researching information. But, only 25% actually purchase their policy online.

The point I'm trying to make is, whatever is congruent for you, do it. What doesn't work with your flow, simply discard it.

Selling over the Phone vs In Person?

From an efficiency standpoint selling over the phone is a no brainer. If you choose to sell over the phone you can achieve a much higher contact rate but you sacrifice effectiveness. You can contact more people more often. The main advantage to meeting in person is that you closing rate dramatically increases. It increases because you can illustrate coverages for purposes of upselling. You can actually see buying signal. It's a lot harder to say no in person rather than over the phone. If someone actually shows up in person it shows they care or have concerns they want a professional to address.

How do I get them into the office?

Depends on the client. For most clients it's tough for scheduling purposes. But, just ask.

Agent: Okay I have most of your info that we need to start looking at some options. Now what's a good time of day to meet morning, afternoon or evening?

Prospect: Can't you explain this over the phone? Or can't you just give me a number?

Agent: I most certainly can. But as a rule for my Agency, I take protecting your assets very seriously and if you have 5 or 10 minutes I would like to sit down with you and your wife (slight pause) and explain how this policy works to protect your assets.

Agent: Bob, I sure can. And I'm sure a lot of Agents will just throw out numbers to try and earn your business. What I've found in my practice is that when it comes to protecting everything you care most about in this world (slight pause) your family… your assets… it's usually better to take 5 or 10 minutes and sit down to evaluate your current protection. (Shut Up and wait for an answer)

Usually you get one of two responses.

Prospect: Okay.

Or

Prospect: I'd rather just do this over the phone.

Even if you don't meet in person at least you made an attempt to meet in person.

Consumer Segmentation

What Percentage of Customers Move Companies Each Year?

From industry research we know the insurance market is about 20% fluid. Which means the average retention for an insurance company is 80%.

What Percentage of Customers Shop Each Year?

There's not an actual definite answer to this question. But, latest research from insurance quotes shows 8% of people shop for insurance multiple times per year, 25% once a year, 27% Every Few Years and 39% never.

Who are the insurance shoppers?

There are 7 types of insurance shoppers, Price Shoppers, Bargain Shoppers, Convenience Shoppers, Relationship Shoppers,

Coverage Shoppers, First Time Consumers, and Vengeance Shoppers. These are categories in my firm we put each client into. Once we knew who we were dealing with it was easier to tailor make our presentation to suit their needs or know whether or not to refer them to another firm.

Price Shoppers – usually a customer in the sub-standard market, higher claims frequency, usually does not understand how insurance works, shops frequently, lower deductibles, etc.

Bargain Shoppers – you'll find these shoppers in any market. Typically they have lower claims frequency but are looking to save money for equal or better coverage.

Convenience Shoppers – Some consumers understand the value of insurance but have policies that are scattered all over the place. They might have so many polices that they do not know what they have exactly. They are looking to simplify and will pay more for it. Other convenience shoppers just want to know as their agent you will 'take care of them'. As their agent they want you to make their life easier.

Relationship Shoppers – These shoppers shop because of an existing relationship. These people usually fall into the category of people who also just want to be cared about. Remember caring is a hot commodity. People love to be around people who care about them.

Coverage Shoppers – Coverage shoppers have assets or aspire to one day have assets and want protection. They want certainty that a claim if filed will be paid and that they are paying for the protection. They understand the value of insurance and appreciate education.

Vengeance Shoppers – These shoppers had a bad experience with a claim, a bad experience with billing or the insurance company and or a bad experience with their agent.

First Time Consumers – Usually a spouse who lost a spouse through passing or divorce and now they have to handle the insurance. A young married couple are first time home buyers. Younger clients who have to purchase insurance for the first time.

But Mike, how do I figure out which shopper I'm dealing with?

Identifying a Price Shopper

Agent: How can we help?

Prospect: "I want/need to pay less for insurance."

Agent: Okay, besides price what do you care about?

Prospect: "I just want the cheapest insurance possible."

Identifying Bargain Shoppers

Agent: How can we help?

Prospect: "I (think or feel) that I'm paying too much for insurance."

Prospect: "We've been reviewing our budget and think we are looking for areas to save."

Agent: Great. The fastest way to save money with insurance is by looking at slightly higher deductibles. How about we bump up your collision from $500 to $1000? (Also opens up bundling options)

Identifying Convenience Shoppers

Agent: How can we help?

Prospect: I've got a lot of insurance and would like to see what's out there.

Agent: Well, let me ask you something Bob, if I could find a way to bundle all of your policies, would that be something you would consider paying a little more for that?

Prospect: Yes, but obviously it depends on how much of an increase.

Identifying Relationship Shoppers

These are friends, family or Co-workers. Maybe a neighbor. Someone who feels that they have somewhat of an obligation to shop based on knowing the Agent. Remember at the end of the day insurance is for the most part a relationship business.

Identifying Coverage Shoppers

Agent: What brings you by today?

Prospect: I'm not sure I have the proper amount of coverage.

Agent: Okay, why do you feel that way? Or better yet when was the last time your Agent reviewed your coverage?

Prospect: When I first signed up 10 years ago.

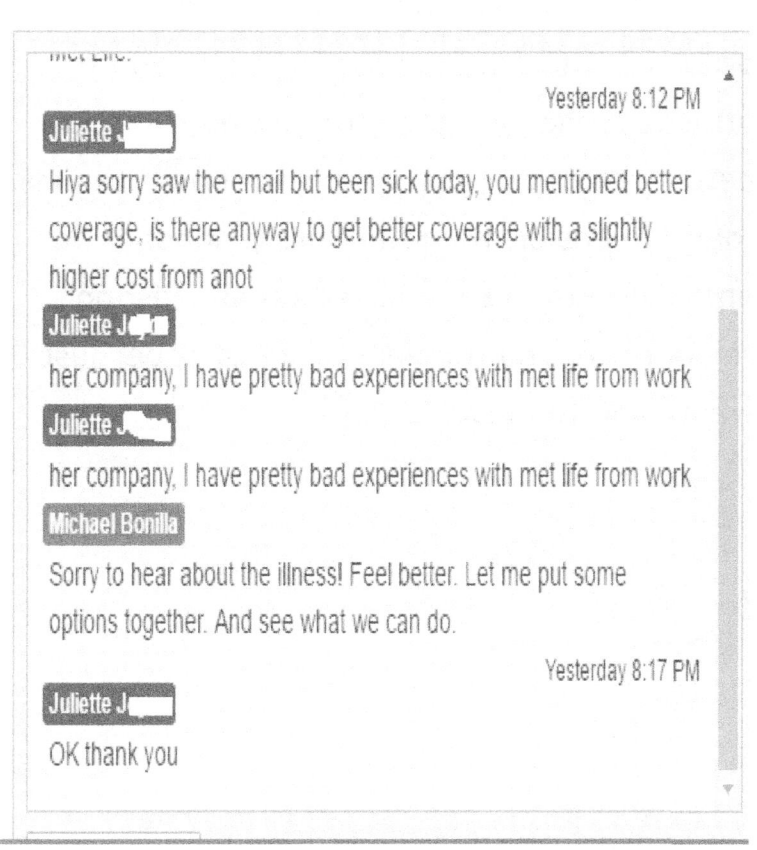

What do all of these consumers have in common?

They are looking for you to solve a problem. The price consumer wants you to provide a cheaper price, the bargain shopper a better value, the convenience shopper to make their life easier, the relationship shopper has an obligation to shop based on an existing relationship and the vengeance shopper just wants you to move.

Marketing

Niche Marketing

Again with Niche Marketing it comes back to what your company can write and what is within your wheelhouse. Here are a few ideas of Niche Marketing:

1. **Previous Loss History Homes**: Homes with loss history are hard to write and lead companies usually offer a discount as Agents for the most part stay away.
2. **Dogs in the Home or Animals**: Most insurance companies stray away from very common dog breeds and can open markets for you. Properties with horses are typically hard to place or Farm Animals.
3. **Home Based Worker**: Clients who have home based businesses often need specialized coverage on their Ho3.
4. **Ride-Share**: Rideshare endorsements are offered by only a handful of

companies. If you happen to represent one think about it as an open market.
5. **Home-Share:** AirBnB and other Home-Sharing companies are becoming extremely popular and are generally hard to place risk.
6. **Targeted Risk Clients:** Ever read the liability exclusions based on profession or famous people? These are people who are targets for liability risk and hard to place.

Here are few interesting marketing/sales figures I found:

1. 48% of sales people never follow-up with a prospect.
2. 25% of sales people make a second contact and stop.
3. 12% of sales people only make three contacts and stop.
4. Only 10% of sales people make more than three contacts.

5. 2% of sales are made on the first contact
6. 3% of sales are made on the second contact
7. 5% of sales are made on the third contact
8. 10% of sales are made on the fourth contact
9. 80% of sales are made on the fifth to twelfth contact.

But Mike, in the age of Internet insurance companies how do I market?

What I found particularly effective was a combination of networking and digital marketing based on our niche. See below for ideas.

Developing Referral Partnerships. Referrals can come from all over, family, friends or strategic partnerships. The best way to ask for a referral is by asking for a referral. If you are sitting down with someone ask if they may know someone who is looking for insurance. Do you happen to know a friend, family member or neighbor who I might be able to help?

Event Marketing. How do you feel about event marketing? To me it was almost my favorite form of marketing. Getting out and meeting complete strangers. I've set up booths at football games, farmers markets, and Chili Cook Off and street fairs. Event marketing is not easy because you really have to put yourself out there for some massive rejection. Event marketing has a relatively low cost once you start going to more and more events.

Ride for Hire? – There was this interesting article in the Insurance Journal back in 2016 talking about an Agency Owner who was UBERing during the day and prospecting her UBER clients.

Transplant Arrangements. We had one of our offices located in an Estate Planning Attorney's office and the other located in a mortgage bank... and you can imagine the potential.

Mike, what about blogging?

Personally I write a lot. I wrote three books on insurance. I write articles for boxing websites for insurance websites. I just enjoy putting words on paper and having conversations with people.

Cold Calling. Cold calling can be a great way to raise your blood pressure. But, for insurance marketing it can be somewhat inconsistent. I take a lot of pride in my cold calling abilities. I once taught a 16 year old with no insurance knowledge to get leads. The problem is that no matter how good of a cold caller you are is that the burn out rate is incredibly high.

Door Knocking. You ever have someone slam the door right in your face? It's not a great feeling and not particularly a great way to market insurance.

Charitable Boards. Joining charitable boards is a great way to build good will and generate an affluent client base. Don't join a board just to get leads. Join a board first and foremost to contribute.

Social Media Marketing. Everyone and there brother is pretending to be the next insurance marketing internet lead generating expert of the week. The truth is there are million dollar lead companies that can't even get it correct. Do you want to go through the time and money to create your own company? Sometimes it makes sense to outsource.

Postcard Mailers. We ran a very inexpensive mailer through an online postcard service and it was wildly successful. We sent out I believe around 100 pieces of mail and received a single response in which we landed a 20+ home client, the total cost was around $134.

Other Marketing Ideas: Fishbowls, Car Wash Ads, Gas Station Ads, Grocery Store Cart ads, Newspaper ads, etc.

YELP and Google Reviews – Our firm was ranked #1 on YELP and it was primarily due to our consistent action and quality service. Consistent in that we asked every single person who bought insurance to review us after signed them up. It generated a tremendous amount of business. Please consider review sites in your marketing efforts.

Internet Leads:

Current Environment: 'Exclusive Internet Leads' are sold sometimes to 3 or 4 Agents and then the data is resold to other lead companies. About 5% of leads are valid if you buy generic leads.

Mistakes Agents Make: Not working leads as soon as they come in and not returning leads when they are not valid leads.

What I've found to work: Firstly, you need a system in place to work the leads. An automated follow up system that connects your phone to the lead or a dialing system. Also, some lead systems connect with your CRM so you can call the prospect with a quote almost in real time.

Remember internet leads is all about the sheer volume and ordering enough to filter out the bad leads. Also, the more specific lead you purchase the less competition you have to deal with.

For instance, for internet leads we had massive success with two lines of business. We had great success with High Risk Home Insurance and Specialty products.

But Mike, People with claims?

Let me ask you something. As an underwriter is a homeowner whose house burned down a bad risk? Yes, of course! Really, why? The home was rebuilt and paid for by the last company. It's a brand new home you are insuring, new pipe, new sprinkler system, new heating and air, new roof. Just one bad day. Could happen to anyone. Obviously, this depends on the negligence of the homeowner for the claim. I actually had insurance companies make me home leads with claims, because no one ever asked for them.

What do you think about Aged lead programs?

Aged leads are great if you have a way to work the leads. All leads are great if you put together a good system for working the leads. Marketing is tough, selling is easy. Marketing takes a tremendous amount of work and follow up.

What do you think about Company Sponsored lead programs?

Great! Take advantage of any internet

traffic you can get your hands on. Internet leads are gold if you know how to work them. Remember, prospecting is about follow up and immediate attempts to contact.

School programs sponsorships:

Every insurance company and their brother wants to market to educators/teachers. Well, find a way to support local schools then.

Here are some ideas:

1. Sponsor a Teacher Appreciation Day at school where you buy something for the break room or bring lunch for the Teachers.
2. Support a sports team at a local school near your office.
3. Frequent school functions with a booth or just as a show of support.
4. Sponsor an Art contest for the school or start an Interact Club.

Networking Groups:

Networking groups are still highly effective ways to drum up business. The best part about networking groups is that most of them are captive, which means they only allow a certain percentage of the same professions.

Another commonly overlooked group would be joining a board of directors for charitable organization.

Here are a few:

1. Rotary International
2. The Elks and Moose Lodge
3. Freemasons
4. BNI
5. Chamber of Commerce
6. Toastmasters
7. Lions

Don't forget to make sure that any board or charity you are pursing has current insurance to protect you from volunteer acts. Or Directors and Officers Insurance.

Lunch and Learns:

People love free food. People love free stuff in general. Lunch and learns are great for higher end clients or for higher premium sales. Annuities or Life Insurance. The reason I always liked lunch and learns was the fact we had a captive audience. Try it sometime.

Cross Selling:

Did you know that 75% of clients will only purchase what you sold them at the first point of sale? Think about it from the prospective of the client. If you didn't sell me the product before, then why do I need it now? Here are some easy ideas. Start by creating a few lists:

1. Auto/No Home
2. Home/No Life
3. Auto/Home/No Life

4. Auto/Home/No Umbrella

Also, if you are looking for life insurance opportunities create lists of clients. For instance, clients turning 55+, clients with expiring term policies, clients who have X-dates within 90 days.

It's important to reach clients about 90 days prior to the renewal as that is generally when the rate increase indications come out.

Another great way to prospect your book of business for life opportunities is looking at clients with recent claims. Someone once said, "Never let a good crisis go to waste."

Up-Selling products:

Up-selling is a great way to add value to clients who may want to fill gaps in their current insurance. Endorsements tend to be very easy to sell for the most part if you can explain why they really need them. What are easy ways to up sell?

Here are some lists that might help you get those creative marketing ideas going:

1. Clients with 100/300/50.
2. Clients with low or no sewer and drainage.
3. Clients with no Home Ins Inflation Rider.
4. Clients with no PAF.
5. Auto No Medical Payments (Quick note on Med Payments, it's the most important and undersold part of an Auto Policy)
6. Clients with Low UMBI.
7. Clients with no collision and no UMPD.
8. Collision no deductible waiver.
9. Collision no rental or low rental.
10. Clients with low deductibles.
11. Clients with no glass buy back deductible.

12. Clients without Gap Coverage
13. Clients who need to schedule Jewelry
14. Clients who own guns.

The Rule of Three

In society we see the rule of three play out. Three signal lights, three Stooges, three blind mice, threes company, three legged stools, awards come in 1st. 2nd and 3rd. So, with my process we focused on three areas. Education, making a professional customized recommendation.

Rule of Reciprocity

The Rule of Reciprocity teaches us that if I give you something you are socially obligated to give me something in return. For instance, if you have questions and I have answers social norms dictate as a prospect you at least listen to my presentation as I helped you with the questions you had.

Rule of Follow the Leader

Ever hear the saying, "Lead, Follow or get out of the way?" People gravitate towards leadership, because leadership provides certainty. We all want to follow people who are similar to us and share similar principles.

As an advisor you are leading people down a journey of discovery and hopefully uncover some truths about their current insurance portfolio. Ask yourself are you someone worth following? Not on social media. In life.

With every sale...

Our job as salespeople is not to tell someone how to think, our job is to give them something to think about. Selling insurance is a search for the truth. Some people are better off staying with their current insurance company/policy or that most people are grossly underinsured. But, the key is we arrive at the truth at the end of every sale.

Using Analogies during the Sales Process

I once was forced to sit through a lengthy Insurance presentation where the agent started to explain leveraged financial assets and compare a strategy to the number of cables on an elevator...

People do not care about your stories and remember that this process can be confusing enough to someone who doesn't have an insurance degree! Keep it simple.

Insurance Jargon

Try to avoid using Insurance Jargon. We have an old industry. Old terms. Non-consumer facing terms. How many people know what a producer is? Or what indemnity means?

Understanding People

How well do you understand people? Understanding people is the key to selling.

People fundamentally operate under the same rule set when dealing with salespeople. They like to do business with people they know, like and trust. If a prospect is uncertain about you, about your product offering, about your agencies ability to handle their needs and or your insurance company, it will most likely kill your sale.

How to leverage Enthusiasm during a sale.

When you are young and don't even know enough to be dangerous enthusiasm can be your best friend. Insurance is boring. Buying insurance is not usually an exciting or fun process. The fastest way to clear out a room of people is by talking about the benefits of a stand-alone umbrella vs a form following umbrella policy. Be excited about what you do but not excited that conveys a sense of desperateness. If you have a cool product feature then talk about it that way. Remember people like showmanship! But, not in a cheesy way.

How People see you...

President Lincoln once refused to add a cabinet member based on his personal appearance. He said, 'Every man over forty is responsible for his face.' Now to me that is a little extreme. But, people do make judgments about us within seconds. The point I wanted to make with this segment is that people will make judgements based on how we dress and how we 'hold' ourselves in public. So, dress for the part and hold yourself with high esteem.

Setting Expectation with Clients Switching a Bargain Shopper or Price Shopper. Flipping the script.

What I've found is that all people buying insurance tend to have three primary concerns.

1. Am I getting a good deal? Price.
2. Will the company pay my claim? Claims Service.

3. Is the enough insurance to protect my assets? Coverage.

What I've also found is that these concerns are all different to different people. So, if you were to rank these from least important to most. Which would be the most important to you? Wait for a response.

But Mike, does that really work?

Yes, try it. I've found that about 25% of price shoppers can be redirected once you uncover and discover their actual areas of concern. With each client segment you are setting expectations. So, if you set the expectation that price is the number one factor for choosing insurance, be vary of the price shopper leaving on renewal if you don't save them money.

What does an insurance sale look like?

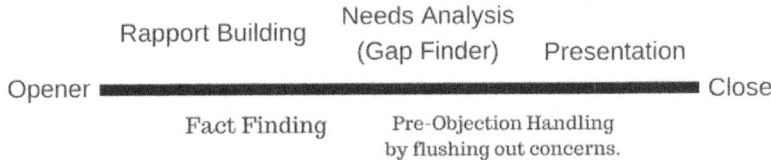

Think of an insurance sale in these simple terms. As we discussed we have two kinds of people. We have think people and feel people. Based on your qualifying process we have determined which people we are dealing with more or less. We have also identified why they are shopping.

As sales people we have these two boundaries. We have a boundary where we bore the person to death with information or we can get them so angry or depressed about insurance they choose to bolt to the nearest exit door. But, all sales follow this process.

They have a beginning and an ending and boundaries we must adhere to.

How do I know when to close a sale?

Before you close you need to know if the customer is ready to be closed. After experience you will know by simply picking up buying signal and the customer will ask buying questions.

Think of a sale like cooking a turkey. You don't shove the turkey into the oven and then turn on the over. It's a front loaded process that requires a lot of preparation. You have to baste the turkey (building rapport), you have to preheat the oven (fact find and qualify) and then you have to cook the turkey (present). And after all that it might come out dry or it might be just right.

With some clients you will know when to close based on buying questions and others will take a little more time in the oven so to speak.

Try to build your presentation style around pre-handling objections and getting to truly understand client needs. The best way to do this is by segmenting the customer into those 6 categories we spoke about earlier of shoppers and then by determining if they are think of feel people so we can tailor make our approach to selling.

How do I know when I crossed a boundary?

The best way is to verify with a question and then proceed or adapt your line of questioning or in the worst case scenario re-establish rapport.

Try these on for starters.

- Lemme ask you John, so far, how does this all sound?

- Lemme ask you something Bob, as a strategy to protect your assets, how does this all sound so far?

Typical Responses

- I think I'd like more information. What does it cost?
- I think it sounds great, let's do this.
- I feel it might be a bit much considering my budget. (Needs more value)
- I feel that could work. (Needs more time)

What we want when selling insurance, is two have the client make one important decision based around two questions. What if they remain under-insured and what happens if they spend a little more money to protect their assets?

Having an Outlet

Ever obsess over something? Your business? Being successful? Writing 4 insurance books in the span of 3 months? It's important to have an outlet to escape from insurance once and a while. For me I like to golf and watch boxing matches.

Inferring Micro Agreements

During your presentation it's important to set expectations and have a process. Part of that process involves inferring micro agreements. For instance, having someone say yes to concepts that build into the final presentation. This is why we talk about taking someone's temperature. Just like cooking, you need to check the thermometer of the meat before you pull it out of the oven. "How does this all sound so far?"

Speaking in Future Tense

As your Agent – speaking in future tense. Learn to speak in the future tense. As your Agent john, my job is to blah blah blah.

Script Example for Internet Lead

Agent: Hi, is Jon home?

Prospect: Yes, this is Jon.

Agent: My name is MB with MGB INS SVS. How you doing?

Prospect: Good. What do you want?

Agent: Great! The reason for the call is that you submitted some info on our website about possibly switching insurance companies. Does that sound familiar?

Prospect: Yes, thanks for calling.

Agent: Great! Like I said I'm Mb with MGB, I'll be your agent helping you through the process. Do you have about 2 minutes?

Prospect: Sure. (Remember they filled out information, people don't tend to do that without expecting to talk with someone)

Agent: Great. I'm going to start working on

some proposals but in the meantime can you send me your declaration page so we can see if you coverage needs to be lowered, remain the same or possible be increased.

Fantastic. When would you have time to come by the office? Does morning, afternoon or evening work best?

When would be a good time for us to swing on by the house and take a look at the property? Does morning, afternoon or evening work best?

What is rapport building?

Traditionally rapport building focusing around talking about someone's family, occupation, etc. And these are all important subjects for qualifying a prospect.

But, true rapport building revolves around establishing yourself as an authority on the subject of insurance. I don't go to the doctor to talk about basketball. But, remember some clients who fall into that relationship bucket will appreciate the extra time talking about interests.

Focus On Value over Price

Price is always a concern but with insurance you are buying peace of mind. You are purchasing a promise. 57% of consumers who call independent agencies do not take the lowest quote provided. Why is that you think?

Because, not all policies are created equal. Because, different consumer segments want different things. Because, sometimes people are just plain under-insured.

What we have also found from industry research is that those same consumers were taking quotes 19% to 53% higher than their current insurance.

Establishing Yourself as an Expert/Authority

Another important rule of selling is establishing yourself as an authority. Your prospect has to know, like and trust you but also understand you know what you are talking about! Every day I read at least 30 minutes of insurance trade info. Thus why I am the most exciting man in the world...

Developing your tools and slick statements.

Not every client is the same. I think I have made that abundantly clear so far. For each client you need to from experience understand who is who and what slick statements work and what questions do not.

Developing your sales process.

Everyone is going to have a different sales process. I've adapted and adopted many different styles and processes into one system.

First build rapport. Second identify why the person is shopping. Third identify what kind of person I am talking to (Think or Feel). Fourth do a needs analysis and qualify. Fifth educate. Sixth design a customized offering to fill gaps. Lastly show how my proposal fills the gaps and close.

When you design your process figure out what works with your flow and your style. What is congruent with the way you present and qualify?

Learning how to Transition Product Lines

Transitioning is moving from one product to the next. So, how do you do that? What you are doing here is asking to ask. For instance:

1. By the way John, who is your X insurance with?

2. Now that we have protected your home and auto, how about we talk about protecting your most valuable asset, your family.
3. Would you mind if we talked about protecting your family.
4. Would you consider paying slightly more per month if we could better protect your assets and family?
5. How do you feel about X insurance?
6. What do you think about Umbrella insurance?

Why do people object?

The root cause of any objection comes down to lack of one of these three key factors, people do business with those they know, like and trust. Remember to build that certainty you have to sell the client on You, Your Product/Service and Your Company.

There are two types of objections:

1. A soft objection
2. An absolute objection

Most people are defensive when it comes to dealing with sales people and most people in general are not agreeable. Some people are too agreeable, but for the most part we are trained to have a wall up to protect us against salespeople. No one wants to be taken advantage of or get stuck with a bad deal. So, sometimes people will give you a soft objection and sometimes you get an absolute no.

Most objections are complaints disguised as objections. If someone says, "That's expensive" I usually say, "You're right." The worst mistake a salesman could ever make is not telling the truth. If you qualify the person from the onset then at the end of your sales presentation you shouldn't encounter many objections, unless they truly cannot afford the offer. It happens.

Most Common Objection Categories:

No Money: I don't think I can afford that.

No Time: I don't have time right now.

No Need: I'm happy with who I'm with.

No trust: I don't know you.

Objection: I've read a lot of bad reviews about XYZ insurance company online.

The truth is, I have as well. I've read bad reviews about every single insurance company. But, what I can tell you is that most people go online to review something just to complain. What really makes the difference when you have a claim is me advocating for you.

Remember, people tend to switch insurance companies for three primary reasons:

- They had a bad experience with their Agent.

- They had a bad experience with their insurance company on a claim or billing situation, and the Agent didn't help.
- They had the wrong insurance policy or amount of coverage and found out the hard way.

Success is not an Accident.

Have a goal. Have a system. Have a vision for what you want to create and stand for as an Agent. Ask yourself some questions:

Do you want to chase price? Do you want to add value? Do you want to be an advisor? Sit down think about why you want to be an insurance advisor. What motivates you? What pushes you? What's your reason why? Why do you want to do this?

Retention

But Mike, Don't people switch because their rate went up?

Yes, some people do. Most people that do this do so because their Agent didn't give them a heads up before the letter got sent out from the insurance company or the Agent didn't do an annual review or the Agent didn't try to find a solution.

How much of the Market is Fluid?

It's estimated that about 20 percent of the insurance market is fluid, more or less. That means 20 percent of your customers will be shopping you each year.

Princeton funded an insurance survey that I found rather interesting. The survey reported that 66% of customers shopped every few years or never over a 13 year period. The study also found that 7% of consumers shopped multiple times per year and about 27% consumers shopped once a year.

Why is retention so important?

Ask yourself, what do you think a

customer acquisition cost is for an insurance customer?

I'd estimate about for every $300 you invest in non-networking based marketing you can expect a single customer. If the average home premium is $1000 and the average commission rate is $150, then you can expect that it takes roughly two years to break even on your marketing investment.

So, if you lose the client in the first year your return on equity will be negative 50% for all of your marketing.

More on Retention

The average captive/independent insurance agency has about an 85% retention ratio. Retention has a lot to do with the value the customer perceives relative to their actual budget.

Action is dictated by perception. Sometimes customers will leave because of a billing issue or something out of your control. It happens.

For Instance, if the rates go up and customer sees no correlation to value there is a high probability that they shop around for a better value.

When a customer shops it's most likely because they received a renewal notice and you didn't bother to call. Agents/Brokers are usually given 90 day notices of a renewal increase. Use that information, don't run from it.

But Mike, how can I hedge my bets?

The simplest way is density per household for PIF. The more policies and endorsements someone has the less likely they are to shop out of sheer laziness. Before sold our business I believe if you include life insurance our average PIF per household was around 4.

Here is a breakdown of the numbers:

1. For a Monoline Auto or Home Policy the average lifespan is 12 month to 14 months.
2. For an Auto and Home Policy the average life span is 18 months to 24 months.
3. For a household with 3 or more polices the average life span is 3 to 5 years.

But Mike, What can I do besides just writing more policies to add value?

Here are some ideas to increase retention based on value:

1. Customer Appreciation BBQ/Cook Outs
2. Thank you cards/calls
3. Claims Follow Up
4. Annual Insurance Review
5. Birthday and Holiday Cards
6. Open Houses

Annual Insurance Reviews:

A big opportunity as an independent agent for me was the fact that the captive insurance agent wouldn't pick up the phone when a client called. This was usually out of fear of a tough conversation or who knows what. I can't tell you how many customers we picked up who said, "My agent never calls me."

Take Note if you are a captive Agency Owner. If you know a rate increase is coming, tell your customer before they get the letter.

Remember people like to be cared about, the simplest way to do that is by showing them you care.

A great opportunity to add some value and help prevent shopping is to sit down with your customer and review their needs on a yearly basis. Wouldn't you rather your customer sit down with you, as opposed to another broker or agent? This is a relationship business at its core, act accordingly.

Don't force a client to meet once a year, simply just ask a question. How often would you (Mr. Customer) like to sit down and evaluate your insurance to make sure we keep everything current?

Part of your qualifying process can be asking this question before you close the sale. As a rule of thumb when it comes to protecting your family, we like to sit down on an ongoing basis to re-evaluate your insurance protection. How often would you like to meet? (Because everyone is different.) Once a year? Twice a year?

Another huge transition we used was this when a prospect had not reviewed their insurance in 5 or 10 years. I'd always be able to tell by looking at the reconstruction cost for a home. "John, when was the last time your agent sat down to review your insurance and make sure it's still current?"

And normally if they were shopping the answer was almost certainly, "When the policy was first written." And usually my response was something to the extent of, "John would it be fair to say that a lot in your life over the past X amount of years has changed?" Or, "Has anything changed in your life in the past X amount of years?" The answer is obvious and would usually result in my ability to compare apples to oranges and sell the correct amount of insurance.

One of the best ways to keep customers is maintaining that face to face trusted advisor role. As a rule of thumb we sat down at least once a year with each of our clients to make sure their assets were not exposed. Life happens and people change. They buy new cards, they change jobs, they buy motorcycles, etc. Sometimes they forget to mention it to you.

Think of it this way, if they are sitting down with you, they are most likely not going to be sitting down with someone else.

Claims follow-up:

As Insurance Agents we sell a promise. It's up to the insurance company to get the insured back to normal. Although we just sell the promise, the Agent can play a big role in how the promise is executed.

I'm not asking you as an Agent to do the work for the insurance company. Even if you're insurance company might be asking, softly.

An Agent has the power of following up throughout the process with the Adjuster and with the insured will add a tremendous amount of value to the process from the insured perspective. One of the key indicators for an insured's level of claims satisfaction is the Agent getting involved as the advocate for the insured. Trust me I did a brief stint as a claims adjuster. Having the agent hold the claims department accountable is paramount to the outcome. Most customers I would speak with who didn't have the agent at least call, would often ask, "What am I paying that guy for?"

Thank you calls:

People crave appreciation and validation. Remind clients that you care about protecting them not just collecting those premium payments and they tend to stick around.

Welcome Packets:

There's something about handing someone something tangible that really adds a lot of value. Especially when we sell an intangible promise. Simply put together a nice welcome packet packed with some business cards, a policy, some magnets, etc.

Birthday Cards:

Birthday calls are important to maintain a proper relationship with clients in any business climate. Think about how many people contact you on your birthday.

Holiday cards:

Holiday cards can be a fun way to showing your clients that you care. Pick one obscure holiday each year to send a card out.

High Probability Sales

Here are the simplest ways to sell insurance with the highest probability of success based on characteristics in the preferred market place. These are also key retention indicators as well.

- High Deductibles, best price point.
- Bundles, harder to switch and shop.
- Method of Payment: EFT, monthly bank draft.
- Higher Limit of Liability

- Meet face to face or in the customers home.
- Customize Coverage based on the need, sell endorsements and benefits.
- Use product comparison to pick apart weaknesses in current offering.

Sales Tips & Rules

Rule Number 1: Don't Complicate Something.

Rule number one of selling insurance is to keep it simple. We are selling insurance not building a space ship. Explain the concepts in digestible terms that consumers can understand and stray away from using too much insurance jargon.

Once I sat thru a long sales consultation with a rep for a large life insurance company. The rep had a well thought out, but thoroughly confusing Indexed Presentation. After about 45 minutes of this rep carrying on I started wondering if she actually was going to talk about how the product actually worked or anything that might be relevant to product features

Rule Number 2: Always be agreeable.

Selling is as much an art as it is a science. There is no formula for agreeableness. Just know that the more confrontational the worse your odds are for closing.

Rule Number 3: Understand the Person.

Don't make snap judgements about what someone can afford. Dig.

There are two types of people that sit in front of you. There are think type of people and feel type of people. What I mean is that people respond to questions in different ways. Some people say, "I think..." and some people say, "I feel..."

The reason why you need to grasp this concept, is the fact that during a sale we have these invisible boundaries. Emotional or feel people require stories and think people require figures and facts. Not everyone is the same. But, there is a limit for feel people and there is a limit for think people that we have to monitor in the sales process.

Rule Number 4: The Person Needs to Understand you.

Ask yourself does the prospect have enough information to know, like and trust me? If not then you need to build that trust through conversation. Through asking questions.

Rule Number 5: Reciprocity

If an insurance sale is a search for the truth we need to follow the rule of reciprocity. The rule of reciprocity makes the insurance buying process a collaborative effort not a confrontational one.

Remember you make no money until the person signs up with you, so you are educating them for free. This is the key to reciprocity. You ask questions to evoke emotions during the process and client has questions that you answer to provide certainty.

The reason why we focused so much on processes in this book is because each sale is more or less always going to be the same. It has an opening and a closing and in between you talk about stuff.

Rule Number 6: Stick to a process.

Every person is different, but every sale is exactly the same. In that, people give you the same responses, the same objections and will follow a path. When you start selling insurance it's important to remember that you have a start, you build rapport, you ask questions that are open ended, you find a problem if one exists, and you build a solution/close.

Feelings Boundary (Feel People)

```
                    Needs Analysis
     Rapport Building  (Gap Finder)    Presentation
Opener ═══════════════════════════════════════════ Close
          Fact Finding    Pre-Objection Handling
                          by flushing out concerns.
```

Information overload (Think People)

Rule Number 7: Know When To Close and Know When to Fold.

Some prospects believe it or not just enjoy talking to sales people and have no intention of buying. Being a salesperson you must think that is somewhat crazy, I did. But, it's true.

During your presentation it's important to know when people are giving off buying signals and asking buying questions.

Think of a sale like a Turkey in the oven. First you have to marinate the turkey. Then you preheat the oven. After your prep work is complete and the oven is at the right temperature you put the Turkey in the oven. Some turkeys require more prep work because some are FROZEN and some are fresh. You cook the turkey and check the temperature along the way. But, you have to keep marinating the turkey as it cooks. If the internal temperature is correct after X amount of hours you pull it out and it's moist. If you leave it in too long it dries out or maybe even burns or becomes ruined.

I'll make an effort to dispense with the food analogies for the rest of the book. Think of it this way. Think of it like an index. The 'Closability' index. Some people are easier to close than others and some require a tremendous amount of effort. But, either way the prospect will ask buying questions.

Well, what's a buying question? For instance, "How much does this cost?" If you are not interested in a product you do not ask how much it will cost. Simple.

Rule Number 8: Ask Open Ended Questions

If you are new to sales or new to insurance. Your best friend is the ability to ask open ended questions and leading questions.

Would you mind if we talked about open ended questions? This is a directive question asking for permission to ask a question.

How do you feel about annuity sales? What do you think about annuity sales? Whatever the answer always remember to ask follow up questions. You have two ears and one mouth so as a ratio ask too questions before you start to babble on about insurance.

Rule number 9: Set Expectations

You need to set boundaries. What should a client come to expect of you? What do you expect of a client?

A lot of Agents (including myself) tell a client that they meet with each client once per year to make sure the insurance is current or on target. There is nothing customized about that statement for a client. Instead why not just ask. How often would you like to meet each year to discuss your insurance? Most of my clients find once a year to meet their needs but some prefer a call once a quarter to check in.

Rule Number 10: Don't lose control of the conversation.

Probably the most common challenge for newer agents is not maintaining focus. A prospect is going to focus on price if you let them and it can derail the conversation.

Price is merely the cost of value. It's your job to educate and present the value. Remember you are the expert and what you focus on will direct the conversation. Don't avoid talking about price, but at the same time don't rush or lead with price. See Diagram Below.

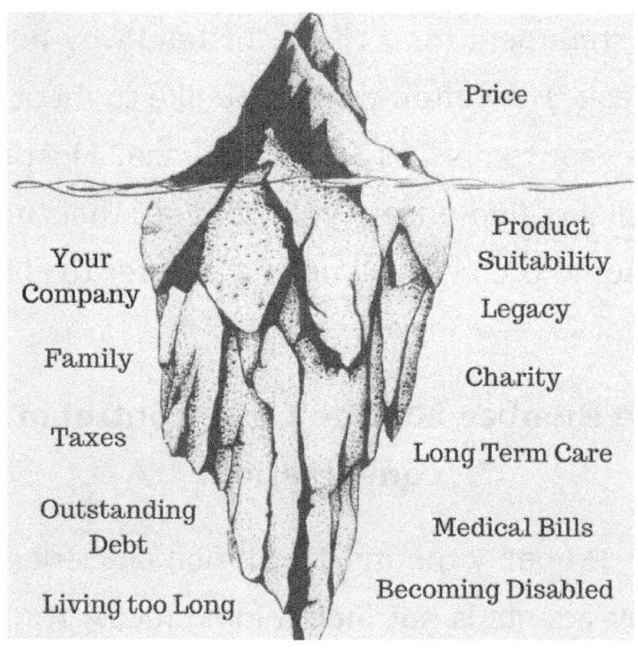

Rule Number 11: Don't always try to reinvent the wheel.

My father was a carpenter and used to say the nail that sticks out tends to get hammered. Craft your approach as you learn your trade. If your trade is selling insurance, then read, apply and learn. It's important as you craft your style/approach to make adjustments. Somethings might work and some might not. But, start by learning from others and adopting an approach and then putting your unique spin on it.

Building Rapport

What do people care about? Why are they buying insurance? If you are prospecting in a social setting what do you do? The biggest problem everyone has when prospecting is being interesting. Most people are not interesting or are worried that they would be the awkward person staring into a cup of whiskey at a mixer. Here are some great questions to instantly get rapport:

1. What do you do for a living? (Talk about someone's occupation/hobbies).
2. How long have you been there?
3. What do you like about it?

4. How'd you get involved in that?

5. What do you do really well?

But Mike, how do you get someone after asking these questions to use your service?

Simple, explain why you care about what you do. Explain your process. Explain your reasons.

Book of Business Valuation

How do I value a book of business? How do I know when I'm overpaying or underpaying? How do I know when the clients will stick with the agency or leave? These are all fairly predictable measures for an insurance agency. Should I use a consultant or purchasing Agency?

But Mike, what if I want to buy an Existing Agency?

There are a couple of options for this. For instance, instead of just going solo and taking a huge gamble. Have you considered a lease to buy agreement? Where you work within the agency for a year and then buy it.

Or where you buy the agency but have the former agent work within the agency for a year to help retention. What are the gross commissions? Any past E&O claims (Errors and Omissions)? Do they have existing processes and systems? Do they have staff in place? The point is to be creative and think outside the dots.

But Mike, how do I value an insurance Agency?

Firstly, you can either buy the book of business (asset purchase) or you can purchase the entire business. Ask key questions. Does the business have employees? Any liabilities? Any Liens? Any DOI (Department of Insurance) complaints? Any carrier contracts that were terminated? A history of the business and clients. Client demographics.

A typical valuation is usually 1X to 2X the agency gross annual commission. Remember the average insurance agency has an 80% retention rate. The averaged purchased agency has an even much lower retention rate. The reason for that is because most transitions happen quickly and sloppily, but also because the customers had a very close relationship with the former agency principle and left because they left.

If you follow baseball at all the big Buzzword still is BA/RISP. It's a way to evaluate how a batter reacts under pressure. Does their batting average fluctuation when it really matters? RISP = runners in scoring position.

If you want to evaluate the BA/RISP for an insurance Agency the key factor for success when looking to buy is PPH or Policies per Household. How many policies does each client have with the agency? The lower the PPH the worse off you will be when acquiring an agency, generally speaking.

The reason why is because the lower policy count per client means lower retention and more work to the agency. The higher amount of policies will determine how 'sticky' your clients are for the most part.

Proper planning is the key to buying an

Agency, because there is a lot of attrition in insurance, especially with mishandled purchases.

With a valuation and purchase you can always be creative. Some Agents are okay with a down payment and having a kicker built in for retention so both parties get a fair deal. First year is a fixed amount payout and the second or third can be variable. There are plenty of insurance consultants who handle purchases and valuations, reach out and speak with one.

Key indicators in the valuation process:

1. How were the clients obtained?
2. What is the Policy Density per Household? (Total Policies per account)
3. Is there a cross-sell program established?
4. What is the Book of Business Retention Rate?

5. What is the growth rate of the Agency? Is the Agency growing or shrinking?
6. What is the average deductible per home/auto?
7. What is the average financial score and or Mileage per auto?
8. Stratification of Liability Limits per Book of Business. How many clients have 15/30, 100/300 and 250/500.
9. What is the average Amount of Insurance per home?
10. Number of Life Insurance Opportunities
11. Number of Upsell opportunities
12. Referral Sources to be Passed On in the Acquisition
13. Infrastructure and Staff
14. What kind of touchpoints does the agency implement?
15. What kind of annual review process has been implemented?
16. Loss Ratio and Claims Filed

17. Does the insurance carrier have an after-hours policy holder's service centre? If so, what is the cost?

How were the clients obtained?

Why is this important? Why does it matter? This business is fundamentally a relationship business and client acquisition can say a lot about the strength of a relationship. I can't tell you how many books of business I've seen wither away after the acquisition because half of the clients were all friends and family of the prior agent.

What is the Policy Density per Household? (Total Policies per account)

Policy Density is the number one indicator of policy retention. Remember this is an odds game. The more policies per account the higher the odds of retaining that account by proxy of sheer density. Insurance companies spend hundreds of millions dollars determining just this. This is why insurance companies push so hard for packages and multiple policies per account. This is also why insurance companies pay higher commissions and leverage profit bonuses based on packaged premium. As a buyer the lower the policy density usually means the lower quality of book of business. This is not always true, because some books can be quality if mono-line home.

Is there a cross-sell program established?

Later in this book we will break down specific cross-selling systems. Why is this important as a buyer? Because, it shows a history of touchpoints and contact attempts. How is the current Agency prospecting the book of business? Have they been berating their members with monthly emails? Do the customers expect to be cross-sold? Cross Selling is one of the easiest revenue generating activities in your agency. Why?

Because, you are prospecting to existing customers with established Agency relationships.

What is the Book of Business Retention Rate?

The average insurance agency has a retention rate of around 85%, depending on the company. The average brokerage is around 90% or so depending on the types of clients. Non-standard books or monoline books usually have retention rates around 70% or so. Is the agency dying or is the agency growing? Which products are growing and which are going?

What is the growth rate of the Agency? Is the Agency growing or shrinking?

In business, in the insurance industry in particular, you are either growing or dying. There is no maintaining, maintaining is an illusion. The larger the agency the smaller the growth rate. Is an agency is growing at 20% or

30%, it might help to know why.

What is the average deductible per home/auto?

Deductibles or self-insured retention is one of the key indicators to the quality of the book of business. Why? Because, it will determine the price sensitivity of clients and how clients view insurance. Do the clients view insurance as a maintenance policy or as insurance? This isn't exactly scientific but books of business with higher SIR will usually on average produce more profitability and higher rates of retention.

What is the average financial score and or Mileage per auto?

Financial Score and Mileage per auto are two key indicators for premium determination for auto insurance policies. The closer the annual mileage is to the state average, the more profitable the book of business. For instance, in California the average mileage per auto is about 13,000 per year. After thorough review some books of business I have seen are closer to 6000 per auto in California.

Stratification of Liability Limits per Book of Business. How many clients have 15/30, 100/300 and 250/500.

If you're planning on purchasing a book of business, know that the limits an agent writes will tell you a lot about the quality of that book. For instance, if you are planning on buying a book of business full over 15/30's or state minimum/liability only policies, you can expect a heavy workload, high staffing requirements and low retention rate.

What is the average Amount of Insurance per home?

When you write a home insurance policy the home will have an Amount of Insurance or AOI. This is the replacement cost of the home or dwelling that you are insuring. What does the amount of insurance say about the book of business? The lower the amount of insurance per client will usually be a key price sensitivity indicator on the book of business. Why is that? Because, at the lower end of the AOI we consistently see more price shopping and higher price sensitivity.

Number of Life Insurance Opportunities

How many clients have life insurance? This is an important question for both density and cash flow determination. The higher number of life insurance opportunities shows a high potential for cash flow the first year you roll the book of business. But, this also can be an indication that the current agent is referring out life insurance to a referral partner who is a life only agent. Find out whether or not the life is being farmed out or referred out, as this will drastically vary your cash flow.

Number of Upsell opportunities

This again is a simple question to answer. For instance, how many clients have low backup sewer and drainage coverage? How many clients only have 100/300 or offset BI/UMBI limits? The number of opportunities to upsell will be a determinate of cash flow the first year. Don't leave money on the table!

Referral Sources to be Passed On in the Acquisition

This is one of the most overlooked questions during the valuation and acquisition of a book of business. Let's say the current agent is receiving 100% of new business from referral sources. Wouldn't it be important to understand what happens to that referral source upon your acquisition of the book of business?

Infrastructure and Staff

Most Agencies are sold as a pure asset purchase, but having an existing staff in play is a huge opportunity as a business owner. Why? Because, you are purchasing a business not just a list of clients.

What kind of touchpoints does the agency implement?

Touchpoints are simply times you touch the client with a communication or attempted communication piece. For instance, welcome letters or welcome phone calls. How often you communicate and how you communicate to clients can make the difference between frustration and disruption or ease of acquisition. For instance, in my firm we focused a lot on texting as it was efficient and more effective than phone calls or emails. Statistically speaking it's just mathematically better as a system. People don't pick up their phone at work, but they read and answer texts (98% of the time open/read). Touchpoints happen in three phases:

1. Before Client Acquisition During Prospecting
2. After Acquisition
3. After Client Departure (lost clients or win-back campaigns)

What kind of annual review process has been implemented?

An annual review is a simple retention system that some agents use and so do not. It's basically a way to get in front of your clients each year and adjust the insurance up or do as needs change. Usually it's a great way to add value and show you are actually an expert not just an order taker.

Loss Ratio and Claims Filed

Loss ratio is maybe the most important rating factor for a book of business. Why? Because, some carriers will cancel your appointment if you consistently lose money or the book of business is not profitable, regardless of size. A profit bonus for most insurance agents is as high as 5% of the GWP. Commission rates range from 10 to 15% of GWP. So, potentially that book of business is lowing upwards of 33% to 50% of potential earning power. For non-standard books this is not a consideration as they usually all lost money.

Does the insurance carrier have an after-hours policy holder's service centre? If so, what is the cost?

Again, this is a simple value add. It's estimated that about 20% of claims are filed after normal business hours. So, if one of all of the companies you represent have this feature, having an after-hours service centre will make your life a lot easier.

Disclaimer

These are not all the factors for weighing a book of business. These are just factors I find useful when I look for potential in a book of business or the quality of a book of business. If you are looking to purchase a book of business or sell a book of business, speak with an expert. CPA and attorney. There are many considerations that vary state by state and will need precise expert valuation to determine.

What do You Need to Get Started?

1. Personal Insurance Licenses (Required)
    a. Completed Pre-license Training

i. From the Department of Insurance, "Pre-licensing Education Applicants for the license types listed in the table below must complete the required hours of General Insurance pre-licensing education and the required hours of Ethics and California Insurance Code as stated below prior to applying for a license. The required hours of Ethics and the California Insurance Code must only be taken once (Section 1749 (g) of the California Insurance Code (CIC)); therefore, applicants applying for more than one license type need not repeat the required hours of Ethics and California Insurance Code*."

- b. Completed Live Scan Background Check
  - c. Pass Exam with a 60% or above.
2. Business Name Check with the DOI (Required)
    - a. You can submit up to 5 names that have to be approved by the DOI prior to having your business licensed. This process can take anywhere from 3 to 5 weeks depending on your DOI.
3. Obtain a Company Insurance License
4. Company Formation (Required if forming as a company)
    - a. LLC Requirements per the Department of Insurance, CA.
        - i. A statement as to the number of licensees rendering professional services on behalf of the LLC.

ii. The LLC must maintain and Errors and Omissions (E&O) policy. Proof of the E&O policy must be provided in the form of evidence of security requirements of financial responsibility naming the LLC as the named insured and/or as an amendment or endorsement to the policy. Additionally, the aggregate dollar amount of E&O Liability Insurance, Cash, Bonds, Bank Certificates of Deposit, U.S. Treasury obligations, and so forth, held to provide security for claims against the LLC must be specified. (The amount required over the minimum of $500,000, is at least

$100,000 multiplied by the number of licensees rendering professional services on behalf of the company; however, the maximum amount is not required to exceed $5,000,000.)
5. Business Insurance (General Liability or Business Owners Policy)
6. City Licenses (Any required City Business License)
7. Surety Bond (Optional Depending on contract type and state)
8. Errors and Omissions Insurance (Required for appointments)
9. DMV Requestor Code (Required)
10. Capital
11. Training
12. Continuing Education

Business Plan

So, you want to start a business? The first step then is to create a business plan. When is the worst time to do your research? After you open the agency. Spend the time now and do your research. This part of the book I'll use a lot of my opinion and some actual examples out of my old business plan.

SWOT Analysis

Create a detailed SWOT (Strengths, Weakness, opportunity, and Threat) for each situation. The first step of creating a SWOT is understanding a SWOT. A SWOT is a breakdown of internal and external factors surrounding a business. A SWOT doesn't have to be elaborate, but a reader should be able to clearly understand your business environment after reading. Why would you want a SWOT? Well, for starters it will help concentrate your marketing efforts and in the event you seek alternative financing a banker might want to look at it.

Internal: Strengths and Weaknesses

External: Opportunities and Threats

Internal

Strengths: My book of business has a 95% retention rate, because of the relationships built, coverages in place and after hours service center. Agency holds a CPCU and CIC designation and has access to 40,000 alumni within local alumni networking, etc.

Weaknesses: Agency has no market for sub-standard home insurance customers or customers with previous liability losses and or water losses. Agency is not open on the weekend or after hours.

External

Opportunities: Local population has grown by 10% in the last year and a large pharmaceutical company has hired about 40,000 employees. Bringing a large educated population that value local advice from a broker/agent.

Threats: ABC Insurance carrier, a local competitor, has recently opened up 5 insurance agencies within 1 mile of your office and invested about $1,000,000 in local advertising.

Questions that you want to ask during the SWOT

What are my commissions? Does this company have a history of lowering commissions? At what point can I receive profit sharing? What does this company do well? What does it need to improve? What do existing agents say?

UVP – Unique Value Proposition

All of my books have the same common theme. Figure out what you do well. Let me ask you, "What do you do really well?" What do you do well in your job? What is the one skill that outshines all of your other skills? What is the one core competency that you can fall back on more than any other competency in your toolset?

Mission Statement. A mission statement is defined as, "A mission statement is a brief summary of an organization's goals and objectives. Most companies, clubs, or nonprofits will have a mission statement indicating commitment and dedication regarding the services they hope to offer."

Examples of Missions Statements

- Apple - A mission statement is a brief summary of an organization's goals and objectives. Most companies, clubs, or nonprofits will have a mission statement indicating commitment and dedication regarding the services they hope to offer."
- Allstate Mission Statement: "To be the best...serving our customers by providing peace of mind and enriching their quality of life through our partnership in the management of the risks they face."

Standards

The hardest part of opening an Agency from scratch was accepting the idea that no every person who walked in the office was a customer. The agency has to have acquisition standards, customer services standards and overall best practices surrounding standards.

It's important to have consistent standards as customers come to expect a certain level of service. This is called your service level agreement and or expectations of a client. Standards should be easily visible to customers and employees. When someone answers the phone at your Agency it shouldn't be a surprise to the person on the other end that you are an insurance Agency. For instance, I was secret shopping an Agency and someone answered the phone, "Hello." Almost unbelievable, right?

Some examples of customer service standards:

- Having a consistent voicemail script
- Having a consistent phone answering script
- Having a consistent email format
- Having a consistent expectation for hours of operation
- Having a consistent email signature

- Having a consistent lead response and follow up system
- Having a consistent claims service follow up

Technology

There are insure-tech firms that have sprung up over the last decade to help you serve your customers better. Some insure-tech firms are competitors and some are value-adds. Generally speaking an Agency has tools at their disposal that rarely if ever get taken advantage of.

- Automated Texting
- Automated Dialing
- CRM / Management System
- Drip Email Systems
- Multi-Rating/Quoting Platform

Motto

Why you need a motto? Because, you own a business. Look give people a reason to remember you. Here are some good examples:

- **Allstate**: You're in good hands.
- **Farmers**: We know a thing or two because we've seen a thing or two.

Vision Statement

Every great business starts with a massive vision. Is being an insurance agent a noble profession? Yes, because we protect people in their time of need. That being said, every great business has a great vision. Take some time and develop your vision statement. Think about what you would like to achieve as a business, what you want to stand for and what kind of mark you want to leave on the industry.

Products Offered

My first business plan had a laundry list of products we sold and offered. Every insurance product that you can imagine and as the agency grew we specialized in purely Auto,

Home and Life Insurance.

Property and Casualty: Auto, Home, Umbrella, Renters, Dwelling Fire (Landlord)

Life and Annuity: Term and Permanent Life Insurance

Customer Focus

The hardest concept I had to accept as an agent licensed to sell 50+ products with over 20 companies, was that not every person that walked in the door was a client.

Our plan is to target college educated homeowners who have kids. Why? Because, that consumer segment values having a trusted advisor, that segment provides us with life insurance opportunities and favorable loss ratios.

Mock Start up Financial Statement

Let's mock up some pro-rata financial forecasting for your Agency. Below you will see a simple excel sheet with a working assumption we are going to work internet leads. We input a fake lead cost, let's say for Preferred Exclusive Auto insurance leads from XYZ lead company. We also assumed we have a captive insurance company and in this state the insurance company closes 14% of quotes and pays 14% on packaged or bundled business. We assumed a mid-premium state average premium.

Premium Forecast and Commission Forecast

Company	Big Captive Insurance Company
State Avg Closing Ratio	14%
Leads Purchased Monthly	500
Lead Cost	$18
Lead Cost Per Month	$ 8,775.00
Leads Per Day	23.80952381
Quoted%	20%
Leads Quoted Per Day	4.761904762
Avg Premium Per Quote	$ 2,500.00
Premium Quoted Per Day	$ 11,904.76
Closted Premium Per Day	$ 1,666.67
Closed Premium Per Month	$ 35,000.00
Quotes Per month	100
Quoted Premium Month	$ 250,000.00
Retention Rate	85%
Commission First Year w/o Life Insurance	$ 46,843.39
Commission Second Year w/o Life Insurance	$ 118,139.32
Commission Third Year w/o Life Insurance	$ 202,199.62

Q1	Q2	Q3	Q4
$105,000.00	$194,250.00	$270,112.50	$334,595.63
Q5	Q6	Q7	Q8
$389,406.28	$435,995.34	$475,596.04	$509,256.63
Q9	Q10	Q11	Q12
$537,868.14	$562,187.92	$582,859.73	$600,430.77

Budget

What is the easiest way to spend more than you bring in? By not looking at your budget. Let's mock up a budget based on my own budget as a scratch agency owner. When you look over this budget the first thing as a new agent you have to consider is whether or not to take a salary. Most agency owners make little to any income the first year in business, because it needs to be reinvested into the business.

	Mock Up		Indsutry Average
Office Rent	1200	7%	10%
Payroll	6000	36%	50%
Accountant	80	0%	1%
Payroll Processing	100	1%	1%
Phone Lines	100	1%	1%
Leads / Marketing	8775	52%	20%
Internet	100	1%	1%
Office Furtniture	100	1%	1%
Computers	50	0%	1%
Other, Misc	250	1%	10%

Carriers Represented

For the sake of this fictitious business

plan we have done our research and will be looking at getting a carrier appointment with "Real Big Insurance Company". Big Insurance Company pays 10% commission on auto insurance for new business and 10% for renewal business. Big Insurance Company also pays 14%/14% for new packaged business. Big Insurance Company has an A+ rating with A.M. Best and consistently has positive customer feedback on claims service.

Staffing Plan

Staffing is one of the most crucial complements to building your business. Most agency owners struggle with staffing. Why? Because, there are many moving parts to deal with. What positions do I hire? What do I pay that person? How do I pay them? How do I hold them accountable? When do I know I can fire someone? When do I know the time is right to hire someone? What the most successful agents will tell you about hiring staff, is that they started hiring as soon as possible. So, let's start by talking about the basics.

Types of Insurance Agency Employees

Insurance has two types of employees. There are employees who do service work or free up time for sales people and there are employees who generate revenue and sell.

These are your typical archetypes or typical roles:

- Producers - Insurance Sales Agents
- CSR – Customer Service Rep
- Marketing Rep
- Agent

Staffing Plan per Policies and Stages

Staffing isn't an exact science. There is no cookie cutter recipe for success. My first staffing plan was to hire as many producers on commission only as possible. Although we started growing quickly my time was bogged down training, hiring and firing. So, that being said, we will break the plan into 3 distinctive growth goals.

Stages for a Generic Growth Plan

- Stage 1: Up to 500 policies or 600,000 GWP (Gross Written Premium)
- Stage 2: Up to 1200 policies or 1.5M GWP
- Stage 3: Up to 1500+ policies or 2.25M GWP

Stage 1: 500 PIF or 600,000 GWP

As you start writing new business and acquiring new clients you will find that your time begins to get bogged down with service work. Such as; changing mortgagee information for a home insurance policy or changing the name of the lien holder on an evidence of insurance. As you grow so will your non-sales related work. As you work your way to 750,000 in premium you'll find a need for some assistance. For some agencies that assistance is needed right away and for others is delayed a bit. For the purposes of our business plan we are going to hire a Part Time CSR to work and do service work for 20 hours per week. We are also going to create an internship program for financial services with my local college to recruit potential producers.

Stages 2 and 3

As you progress the plan is to hire according to needs and capacity. Each employee will have a different productive capacity and should be thought of in the terms of profitability. When we refer to capacity and demand on employees, a typical CSR can handle and manage about 2000 to 3000 policies depending on the type of business. For commercial or business insurance the amount of policies will most likely be much smaller.

CSR – Customer Service Rep

What does a CSR do? It depends on what you want them to do. Typically a CSR handles inbound phone calls, quotes new business, handles customer related billing and claims issues, any outstanding service work, renewal remarketing and trains/manages staff.

How do you pay a CSR? Focus on what result you want. People are people at the end of the day and for the most part we all operate in our best interest. The key mistake I see most insurance brokers/agents make is not having a variable component to their pay schedule for CSR's.

CSR Retention Bonus

A variable pay schedule could be as simple as retention bonus for 85, 90 and 95+ in retention rates / renewal ratio. For instance;

- At 85% retention the CSR gets a monthly bonus of $150.

- At 90% retention the CSR gets a monthly bonus of $200.
- At 95% retention the CSR gets a monthly bonus of $300.

Most Agents who use a standard hourly rate find that their CSR is always 'swamped' with work and retention is inconsistent.

PTO Bank Bonus Program

Another effective bonus program for CSR's is a PTO bank, to implement you need to check with your lawyer. But, a PTO bank works this way. For every 10 umbrella policies a CSR sells they get a PTO day as a bonus. Not everyone is motivated by money, some people love to have days off, I do. Why would this work? Well, 10 umbrellas would be roughly $350 in commission total, probably more than the cost of a day off for a CSR. More importantly, for this to happen it requires the CSR proactively reaching out to your current book of business and upselling, and not to mention your retention goes up by proxy of policy density.

CSR and Commission

The biggest mistake I see agents make is not paying commission for sales. What possible motivation would a CSR have to sell a policy if you don't pay commission? Or what motivation would they have if you pay a straight fee regardless of the price.

CSR Licensing and Appointment

Remember, to pay commissions you need a license. So, should you get your CSR licensed? For my firm we appointed every SSR and got them licensed. Part for E&O purposes but mostly because of how contract law works and agency law.

Choosing an Office Location

Retrospectively starting an Insurance Agency out of my home office wasn't a great business model... But, it worked out in the long run.

If you end up going the captive agency route then talk to your company management about sourcing locations. Captive models have restrictions generally as to where an Agent can start an office. It mostly depends on proximity of other agencies in the local market.

Also, some captive agencies can get low interest rate loans from the parent captive company if they plan on buying the actual building where the agency will be located. Go visit some agencies and get a good feel for what you like.

For this business plan location: Thousand Oaks, CA

We are going to lease an office space in a warehouse in central Thousand Oaks, CA. This will give us the most bang for our buck and allows us to scale as we hire.

Choosing an Office Layout

What should a client/employee see when they walk in the door? What does that say about the place you work and the type of business a customer can expect to be doing business with? There is also a science to laying out an office. Where you place your awards, what a client sees or hears when walking into your office.

Marketing plan

New Business Marketing Plan

- Robust Referral System –ASK, ASK, ASK Again.
    - Ask every client and prospect. "Do you happen to know any friends, co-workers or family members that need help with their insurance?"
- Consistent ask for online reviews.

- o Do you use Yelp, Google reviews, XYZ review?
- o If yes, ask for a review.
- o If no, don't ask.
- Win-Back Campaigns (Lost Clients)
  - o How's life email?
    - Set up automated drip email campaign, asking how the client is liking their new insurance company.
    - Emails sent once, every 9 months or so.
- Quotes Not Closed (Clients not sold)
  - o If you quote a prospect and they drop off or do not sign up, set up a system follow up process to reconnect with them.
    - Follow up Email 7 days out.
    - Follow up Email 14 days out.
    - Follow up Email 30 days out.
    - Follow up Email 60 days out.
    - Follow up Text 8 months out.

- Follow up Call 9 Months out.

Cross Selling Systems

- METC (Send a Welcome Letter Mail Piece at 7 days, send an email at 10 days, send an automated follow up text at 15 days, and call at 30 days). This is a great, simple system an Agent taught me recently.
- Account Rounding Lists
    - Working account rounding lists are the easiest ways to upsell or cross sell. For instance, periodically working Auto/No Home lists or Home/No Auto lists to cross sell.
    - "By the way CLIENT, who is your home insurance with?"
- 90 Day Renewal Account Rounding
    - Rate increase notifications are sent to clients 90 days prior to renewal. This is the perfect time to try and maximize their insurance purchase

and round the account or cross sell and or upsell coverages.
- Ask and you shall receive: Life Cross Sell Program
    - After every sale, ask, "BY the way who is your life insurance with?"

Retention Plan / Remarketing Plan

- Process
    - Call 90 days prior to renewal date.
        - Combat Rate increases by moving up deductibles.
    - Explain the rate increase or decrease.
        - Explain the marketplace and rate increases and history of increases.
    - See if the client wants to stay with current company.
    - Shop policy and remarket.

Value Added Systems

- Claims Follow Up
    - Statistically the number one driver for a positive claims experience is the Agent asking to get involved.
    - Ask the client how the claims experience is going at the onset and at closing.

Target Demographic Market Analysis

Location: Thousand Oaks, CA

Population: 128,000

Median Age: 42.8

Married: 60%

Median Home Price: $669,000

Income per Household: $100,000

Average Premium per Household: Estimated $2500 per household

Average Life Insurance Ownership: 70%

Average Miles Driven: Commute 30 miles per day

Average AOI per home: 400,000

Historical Loss Ratio: Favorable, high

profitability from a loss ratio standpoint. Proximal Insurance Agencies: about 100 local agents within 5 miles of Thousand Oaks.

Continuing Education Plan

How do you plan on educating your staff? When we stop learning we stop growing. How do you get your CSR to sell? The first part we addressed and that was starting with variable compensation structure for pay schedules but it will also require dealing with the fact that CSR's have sales aversion. That's right, often CSR's feel that, "They don't want to be perceived as a salesperson."
Here are some simple ideas:
- Weekly Sales Training Meetings for 30 minutes
- One on One Sales Training
- Role Playing as needed
- Webinars
- Mastermind Groups

- Designations and On-going licensing

Summation

I try to keep these books short and to the point. If you enjoyed the read and want to help support my weekend golf excursion please leave a review.

Made in the USA
Monee, IL
03 April 2025

15102523R00100